MW01601434

Vegan Instant Pot Cookbook

Healthy and Delicious Plant-Based Recipes for Your Pressure Cooker

Jasmine King

The trademarks that are used are without any consent, and the publication of the trademark is without permission or backing by the trademark owner. All trademarks and brands within this book are for clarifying purposes only and are owned by the owners themselves, not affiliated with this document.

Table of Contents

Introduction 1

CHAPTER ONE.. 3

Vegan Instant Pot Recipes for Beans 3

    Charro Beans 3

    Vegan Baked Beans 5

    Instant Pot Pinto Beans.................................7

    Black Beans and Rice.................................... 8

    Rajma Red Kidney Beans 9

    Fagioli al Fiasco 11

    Vegan Chickpea Curry 13

    Munggo 15

    Red Lentil Chili..................................... 17

    Lentil Tacos... 19

    Spicy Chili 20

CHAPTER TWO 22

Vegan Instant Pot Recipes for Grains 22

    Pea and Celery Risotto................................22

    Butternut Squash Risotto 24

    Mexican Polenta 26

    Israeli Couscous......................................27

    Brown Rice Pilaf 28

    Creamy Oats 29

    Pumpkin Pie Sorghum.................................. 30

    Instant Quinoa....................................... 31

    Mac and Cheese 32

    Brown Rice..34

    Vegan Buckwheat Porridge 35

    Brown Rice & Green Tea Porridge 36

Multigrain Porridge 37

CHAPTER THREE **39**

Vegan Instant Pot Recipes for Soups.....................**39**

Carrot and Sweet Potato Soup.............................. 39
High Fiber Vegetable Soup 41
Wild Rice Soup.. 43
Creamy Broccoli Soup... 45
Chard, Lentil and Potato Soup 47
Butternut Squash Soup... 49
Corn and Red Pepper Chowder 51
Vegan Lasagna Soup 53
Coconut Chickpea Curry 55
Hot and Sour Soup.. 56
Split Pea Soup 57
Vegetarian Minestrone Soup 58

CHAPTER FOUR **61**

Instant Pot Recipes for Vegetables **61**

Garlicky Bell Peppers..61
Vegetable Mélange.. 63
Eggplant Italiano 65
Veg Chow Mein 66
Spiced Okra 67
Spinach with Tomatoes.. 68
Quinoa with Mushrooms and Peppers 70
Vegetable Curry with Tofu.................................... 72
Vegetable Succotash 74
Cabbage with Carrot 76
Cauliflower Bolognese with Zucchini Noodles.......77
Barbecued Tofu and Vegetables 79
Green Bean Warm Salad..81
Beets and Garlic Sauté 83
Tangy Sweet Potato Wedges................................. 84

CHAPTER FIVE **86**

Vegan Instant Pot Recipes for Desserts **86**

    Pumpkin Date Pudding 86

    Chai Spiced Pears 88

    Coconut Rice Pudding 89

    Pear and Cranberry Cake 90

    Apple Crumble...92

    Buckwheat Pudding..93

    Cranberry Stuffed Apples 94

    Tapioca Pudding 95

    Fresh Berry Compote..96

    Cashew Lemon Cheesecake................................97

Conclusion **99**

Check Out My Other Books **100**

Introduction

The Instant Pot is a programmable electric pressure cooker that is sure to revolutionize your cooking experience forever. In addition to pressure cooking, it can be used as a slow cooker, rice cooker, stove, steamer, yogurt maker, and sauté pan. Using an Instant Pot, you can prepare delicious meals in less than 15 minutes without worrying if you have the right kitchen appliances for it.

Veganism tries to actively curb animal exploitation and cruelty. People tend to opt for a vegan diet due to ethical, environmental, or health concerns. A vegan diet is devoid of all animal-based products, which include meats, poultry, eggs, fish, and dairy products. It offers various health benefits including weight loss, lower blood sugar, improved heart health and kidney function.

If you follow the vegan diet, learning to prepare vegan recipes is an important step towards achieving your goals. In this book, you will find 61 easy and delicious vegan Instant Pot recipes for beans, grains, soups, vegetables, and dessert.

CHAPTER ONE

Vegan Instant Pot Recipes for Beans

Charro Beans

Serves: 4
Cooking Time: 40 minutes
Ingredients:
½ tablespoon olive oil
1 small jalapeño, chopped
½ pound pinto beans, rinsed
½ teaspoon cumin powder
1 small onion, chopped
2 cloves garlic, minced
3 cups water
Salt to taste
A handful of fresh cilantro, chopped

Directions:
1. Press the SAUTÉ button. Add oil. When the oil is heated, add onion, garlic, and jalapeño. Sauté until onion turns translucent.
2. Add beans, cumin, and water. Mix well. Press the CANCEL button.
3. Close the lid. Select the BEAN/CHILI button and set the timer for 30 minutes.
4. When the timer goes off, let the pressure release naturally.
5. Stir and add salt to taste.
6. Garnish with cilantro and serve.

Nutritional Information (Per Serving)
Calories: 224

Fat: 2.6 g
Sat Fat: 0.4 g
Carbohydrates: 38.2 g
Fiber: 9.5 g
Sugar: 2.2 g
Protein: 12.7 g

Vegan Baked Beans

Serves: 4
Cooking Time: 45 minutes
Ingredients:
½ pound navy beans
1 small onion, diced
½ tablespoon olive oil
2 cloves garlic, minced
1 small jalapeño, chopped
1 green bell pepper, chopped
3 ounces tomato paste
2 tablespoons molasses
1 cup low sodium vegetable broth
1 cup water
½ tablespoon yellow mustard
1 tablespoon maple syrup
Salt and pepper to taste
⅛ teaspoon smoked paprika
½ teaspoon apple cider vinegar
A handful of fresh cilantro, chopped

Directions:
1. Soak the beans in a bowl of hot water for at least an hour. Drain and rinse the beans.

2. Press the SAUTÉ button. Add oil. When the oil is heated, add onion, garlic, jalapeño, bell pepper and salt. Sauté until onion turns translucent.

3. Add beans and water. Mix well. Press CANCEL.

4. In a bowl, mix together broth, molasses, tomato paste, mustard, maple syrup, paprika, vinegar, and pepper and pour into the Instant Pot. Mix well.

5. Close the lid. Select MANUAL and cook at high pressure for 30 minutes.

6. When the timer goes off, let the pressure release naturally.

7. Garnish with cilantro and serve.

Nutritional Information (Per Serving)
Calories: 292
Fat: 2.9 g
Sat Fat: 0.4 g
Carbohydrates: 55.3 g
Fiber: 15.8 g
Sugar: 16.2 g
Protein: 14.5 g

Instant Pot Pinto Beans

Serves: 4
Cooking Time: 30 minutes
Ingredients:
½ pound dry pinto beans, rinsed
2 cups vegetable broth
¾ cup water
Salt and pepper to taste

Directions:
1. Add all the ingredients into the instant pot.
2. Close the lid. Select MANUAL and cook at high pressure for 30 minutes.
3. When the timer goes off, let the pressure release naturally.
4. Stir and serve.

Nutritional Information (Per Serving)
Calories: 216
Fat: 1.4 g
Sat Fat: 0.3 g
Carbohydrates: 35.9 g
Fiber: 8.8 g
Sugar: 1.6 g
Protein: 14.6 g

Black Beans and Rice

Serves: 4
Cooking Time: 45 minutes
Ingredients:
1 cup brown rice, rinsed
1 cup black beans, rinsed
2 tablespoons olive oil
2 cloves garlic, minced
1 medium onion, chopped
Salt to taste
2 teaspoons lime juice
4½ cups water
½ avocado, sliced to serve

Directions:

1. Add all the ingredients except lime juice and avocado into the Instant Pot.

2. Close the lid. Select MANUAL and cook at high pressure for 25 minutes.

3. When the timer goes off, let the pressure release naturally.

4. Open the lid and fluff with a fork. Add lime juice and stir.

5. Spoon into bowls. Garnish with avocado slices and serve.

Nutritional Information (Per Serving)
Calories: 463
Fat: 13.9 g
Sat Fat: 2.5 g
Carbohydrates: 71.9 g
Fiber: 11.3 g
Sugar: 2.4 g
Protein: 14.9 g

Rajma Red Kidney Beans

Serves: 6
Cooking Time: 40 minutes
Ingredients:
2 cups dry kidney beans, soaked in water overnight and drained
2 tablespoons vegetable oil
2 large onions, chopped
1 teaspoon ginger paste
1 teaspoon garlic paste
½ teaspoon turmeric
1½ teaspoons ground cumin
Chili powder to taste
1 teaspoon garam masala (Indian spice blend)
2 teaspoons ground coriander
3 large tomatoes, chopped
Water
Salt to taste
Cilantro to garnish

Directions:
1. Select SAUTÉ. Add oil. When the oil is heated, add onions and sauté until light brown.
2. Add ginger and garlic pastes and sauté for 2–3 minutes.
3. Add turmeric, cumin, coriander, garam masala and chili powder and sauté for a few seconds.
4. Add tomatoes and sauté for 2 minutes. Press CANCEL.
5. Add kidney beans, stir, and add enough water (2 inches above the ingredients) and salt.
6. Close lid. Select the BEAN/CHILI button and set the timer for 30 minutes.

7. When the timer goes off, let the pressure release naturally.

8. Garnish with cilantro. Serve over rice.

Nutritional Information (Per Serving)
Calories: 293
Fat: 5.9 g
Sat Fat: 1.1 g
Carbohydrates: 47.2 g
Fiber: 11.8 g
Sugar: 5.9 g
Protein: 15.6 g

Fagioli al Fiasco

Serves: 4
Cooking Time: 20 minutes
Ingredients:
For the beans:
½ pound borlotti beans, soaked overnight and drained
3 tablespoons olive oil
3 cups water
3 medium sage leaves
½ teaspoon sea salt
3 cloves garlic, smashed
¼ teaspoon crushed red pepper flakes
1 cup kale, chopped

Optional garnishing: Use any or all of them
Fresh herbs of your choice, chopped
Lemon wedges
Pickled red onions
Scallions

Directions:
1. For the beans, all the ingredients except kale into the Instant Pot.
2. Close the lid. Select MANUAL and cook at high pressure for 20 minutes.
3. When the timer goes off, let the pressure release naturally for 10 minutes. Quick release the remaining pressure.
4. Add kale and stir. Close the lid and set aside for some time until the kale wilts.
5. Serve beans in serving bowls. Place the garnishing on top.

Nutritional Information (Per Serving)

Calories: 293
Fat: 11.3 g
Sat Fat: 1.7 g
Carbohydrates: 36.9 g
Fiber: 14.5 g
Sugar: 0 g
Protein: 13.8 g
Sodium: 250 mg

Vegan Chickpea Curry

Serves: 3
Cooking Time: 10 minutes
Ingredients:
1 tablespoon olive oil
1 can (15 ounces) chickpeas, rinsed and drained
½ cup vegetable broth
7½ ounces canned crushed tomatoes, with its juice
½ green bell pepper, chopped
½ cup frozen corn
1 cup kale leaves, chopped
½ cup okra, sliced
½ cup frozen green beans
2 cloves garlic, minced
¾ cup onions, chopped
½ tablespoon maple syrup
2 teaspoons curry powder
⅓ cup fresh cilantro, chopped, to garnish
Salt to taste

Directions:
1. Press SAUTÉ. Add oil. When the oil is heated, add onion and sauté until translucent. Add bell pepper and garlic and sauté for a couple of minutes.

2. Add rest of the ingredients and stir. Press CANCEL.

3. Close the lid. Select MANUAL and cook at high pressure for 5 minutes.

4. When the timer goes off, let the pressure release naturally.

5. Add cilantro and stir. Serve hot over rice.

Nutritional Information (Per Serving)
Calories: 342
Fat: 6.2 g

Sat Fat: 0.8 g
Carbohydrates: 57.8 g
Fiber: 17.5 g
Sugar: 24.5 g
Protein: 16.3 g

Munggo

Serves: 8
Cooking Time: 7–8 minutes
Ingredients:
2 cups dry mung beans, soaked in water for 8 hours, drained
1½ cups water
2 teaspoons olive oil
4 cloves garlic, minced
1 large onion, sliced
2 cups tomatoes, diced
5 cups fresh baby spinach
Salt to taste
½ teaspoon chili powder (optional)
2 teaspoons curry powder
2 tablespoons lime juice

Directions:
1. Select SAUTÉ. Add oil. When the oil is heated, add onions and garlic, and cook until the onions are translucent.

2. Add tomatoes and cook for a couple of minutes.

3. Add salt and mung beans. Mix well and add water. Press CANCEL.

4. Close the lid. Select MANUAL and cook at high pressure for 7–8 minutes.

5. When the cooking is complete, let the pressure release naturally.

6. Open the lid carefully, add spinach, chili powder and curry powder. Stir and keep it covered for 5 minutes.

7. Add lemon juice. Mix well and serve.

Nutritional Information (Per Serving)
Calories: 217
Fat: 2.1 g

Sat Fat: 0.4 g
Carbohydrates: 38.4 g
Fiber: 10.1 g
Sugar: 5.7 g
Protein: 13.7 g

Red Lentil Chili

Serves: 10
Cooking Time: 20 minutes
Ingredients:
5 cups red lentils
5 cups water
6 large tomatoes, chopped
2 red bell peppers, chopped
1 cup pitted dates
1 teaspoon oregano
1 teaspoon salt
1 teaspoon chili flakes
2 tablespoons apple cider vinegar
2 teaspoons paprika
4 garlic cloves, minced
2 large onions, chopped
¾ teaspoon chipotle powder

Directions:
1. Add tomatoes, garlic, red bell pepper, dates, and one cup of water to a blender and blend until smooth.

2. Add remaining items to the Instant Pot and mix well.

3. Add the date mixture to the pot and cover the lid. Cook at high pressure for 15 minutes.

4. When the cooking is complete, do a natural pressure release for 10 minutes. Quick release the remaining pressure.

5. Remove from the pot and serve hot.

Nutritional Information (Per Serving)
Calories: 433
Fat: 1.5 g
Sat Fat: 0.2 g
Carbohydrates: 80.8 g
Fiber: 33.3 g
Sugar: 18.7 g

Protein: 26.9 g
Sodium: 252 mg

Lentil Tacos

Serves: 4
Cooking Time: 25 minutes
Ingredients:
1 cup lentils, rinsed
2 ounces tomato sauce
2 cups water
1 onion, chopped
4 cloves garlic, minced
1 teaspoon smoked paprika
1 teaspoon chili powder
Salt and pepper to taste
Taco shells
Toppings as per your choice such as lettuce, tomatoes, and salsa.

Directions

1. Add lentils, water, garlic, paprika and chili powder to the Instant Pot.

2. Close the lid. Select MANUAL and cook at high pressure for 25 minutes.

3. When the cooking is complete, let the pressure release naturally.

4. Add salt and pepper and stir.

5. Stuff in taco shells along with the toppings of your choice and serve.

Nutritional Information (Per Serving)
Calories: 192
Fat: 0.8 g
Sat Fat: 0.1 g
Carbohydrates: 33.8 g
Fiber: 15.9 g
Sugar: 2.9 g
Protein: 13.2 g

Spicy Chili

Serves: 4
Cooking Time: 4 minutes
Ingredients:
1 tablespoon oil
½ cup onions, chopped
Red pepper flakes to taste
½ pound veggie burger crumbles (optional)
½ tablespoon ground cumin
1 bay leaf
1 cup vegetable broth
½ tablespoon red wine vinegar
8 ounces canned kidney beans, drained, rinsed
8 ounces canned pinto beans, drained, rinsed
14 ounces canned black beans, drained, rinsed
3 cloves garlic, minced
½ tablespoon chili powder
1 teaspoon oregano
14 ounces canned diced tomatoes
3 ounces tomato paste
Salt to taste

To garnish:
Chives, chopped

Directions:
1. Select SAUTÉ. Add oil. When the oil is heated, add onion, garlic, red pepper flakes and veggie burger crumbles and sauté until onions are translucent.

2. Add chili powder and cumin and sauté until fragrant. Press CANCEL.

3. Add rest of the ingredients and stir.

4. Close the lid, select MANUAL, and cook at high pressure for 4 minutes.

5. When the cooking is complete, do a quick pressure release.

6. Ladle into bowls. Garnish with chives and serve.

Nutritional Information (Per Serving)
Calories: 387
Fat: 7.4 g
Sat Fat: 1.2 g
Carbohydrates: 61.3 g
Fiber: 14.8 g
Sugar: 8.6 g
Protein: 22 g

CHAPTER TWO

Vegan Instant Pot Recipes for Grains

Pea and Celery Risotto

Serves: 6
Cooking Time: 10 minutes
Ingredients:
6 tablespoons olive oil
2 medium onions, chopped
4 celery sticks, chopped
1 teaspoon pepper powder
Salt to taste
2 cups Arborio rice, rinsed
4 cloves garlic, minced
4 cups vegetable broth
2 cups frozen green peas
Zest of 1 lemon, grated

To garnish:
4 tablespoons lemon juice
2 ounces nutritional yeast

Directions:
1. Select SAUTÉ. Add oil. When the oil is heated, add onions, salt, pepper, and celery, cook until the onions are translucent.
2. Add rest of the ingredients and mix well. Press CANCEL.
3. Select the RICE button. When the rice cycle completes, open the lid.

4. Add nutritional yeast and lemon juice. Stir and serve right away.

Nutritional Information (Per Serving)
Calories: 515
Fat: 15.9 g
Sat Fat: 2.5 g
Carbohydrates: 81.4 g
Fiber: 5.1 g
Sugar: 22.1 g
Protein: 11.9 g

Butternut Squash Risotto

Serves: 4
Cooking Time: 12 minutes
Ingredients:
1 tablespoon vegetable oil
1 white onion, finely chopped
1 red bell pepper, chopped
3 garlic cloves, minced
1½ cups risotto rice
3½ cups vegetable broth
1 cup chopped button mushrooms
2 cups butternut squash, peeled and diced
3 cups of assorted greens (spinach, kale, and chard)
Salt and pepper to taste
1 tablespoon nutritional yeast

Directions:
1. Heat the vegetable oil in the Instant Pot on SAUTÉ.
2. To this, add minced garlic, onions, and chopped bell pepper, and sauté until they turn slightly soft.
3. Throw in the risotto rice and stir well.
4. Pour the vegetable broth into the pot, followed by chopped mushrooms, butternut squash, greens, salt, and pepper, and mix well.
5. Cover the lid and cook at high pressure for 7 minutes.
6. When the cooking is complete, do a natural pressure release for 10 minutes. Quick release the remaining pressure.
7. Transfer the risotto to the bowls. Sprinkle nutritional yeast on top and stir. The mixture will thicken shortly, and be ready to serve.

Nutritional Information (Per Serving)
Calories: 410
Fat: 5.5 g

Sat Fat: 0.8 g
Carbohydrates: 77 g
Fiber: 4.9 g
Sugar: 5.2 g
Protein: 13.8 g

Mexican Polenta

Serves: 4
Cooking Time: 10 minutes
Ingredients:
1½ cups corn grits
1 tablespoon olive oil
3 teaspoons garlic, minced
1½ cups green onion, sliced
⅓ cup cilantro, chopped
3 cups boiling water
3 cups vegetable broth
2 teaspoons oregano
1 teaspoon cumin
1½ teaspoons chili powder or to taste
¼ teaspoon cayenne
¾ teaspoon smoked paprika
Salt to taste

Directions

1. Select SAUTÉ. Add oil. When the oil is heated, add green onion and garlic and sauté until fragrant.

2. Add rest of the ingredients and stir. Press CANCEL.

3. Close lid. Select MANUAL and cook at high pressure for 5 minutes.

4. When the timer goes off, let the pressure release naturally for 10 minutes. Quick release the remaining pressure.

5. Mix well and serve.

Nutritional Information (Per Serving)
Calories: 145
Fat: 5.7 g
Sat Fat: 1 g
Carbohydrates: 18.8 g

Fiber: 3.1 g
Sugar: 1.9 g
Protein: 6.5 g

Israeli Couscous

Serves: 5
Cooking Time: 5 minutes
Ingredients:
8 ounces Harvest grains blend
1½ cups vegetable broth
1 tablespoon olive oil
Salt and pepper to taste

Directions:
1. Select SAUTÉ. Add oil. When it heats, add broth and Harvest grains blend and stir. Press CANCEL.
2. Close the lid. Select MANUAL and cook at high pressure for 5 minutes.
3. When the timer goes off, quick release the pressure.
4. Fluff with fork. Season with salt and pepper and serve.

Nutritional Information (Per Serving)
Calories: 324
Fat: 6.4 g
Sat Fat: 0.5 g
Carbohydrates: 64.3 g
Fiber: 9 g
Sugar: 0.2 g
Protein: 14.2 g

Brown Rice Pilaf

Serves: 4

Cooking Time: 20 minutes

Ingredients:

2 teaspoons coconut oil

1 medium onion, chopped

1 cup mushrooms, sliced

1 clove garlic, finely minced

1 cup wild rice and brown rice medley, rinsed and drained

1½ cups vegetable broth

Salt and pepper to taste

A handful fresh parsley, chopped

Directions:

1. Select SAUTÉ. Add oil. When the oil is heated, add onion and mushroom and sauté for 3–4 minutes.

2. Stir in the garlic and sauté until fragrant.

3. Stir in rice and sauté for 2–3 minutes. Stir constantly. Press CANCEL.

4. Add the broth. Scrape the bottom of the pot to remove any browned bits that may be stuck.

5. Close the lid. Select the MULTIGRAIN button and set the timer for 20 minutes.

6. When the timer goes off, let the pressure release naturally.

7. When done, fluff with a fork. Sprinkle with salt and pepper and garnish with parsley and serve.

Nutritional Information (Per Serving)

Calories: 261

Fat: 5.6 g

Sat Fat: 2.8 g

Carbohydrates: 40.6 g

Fiber: 2.5 g
Sugar: 2.9 g
Protein: 11.4 g

Creamy Oats

Serves: 4
Cooking Time: 3 minutes
Ingredients:
1½ cups steel cut oats
A pinch salt
1 cup coconut milk
3½ cups water
½ teaspoon ground cinnamon
Toppings of your choice such as fruits and nuts

Directions:
1. Add oats and water into the Instant Pot.
2. Close the lid. Select MANUAL and cook at high pressure for 3 minutes.
3. When the timer goes off, let the pressure release naturally.
4. Add cinnamon and stir. Let it cool for a few minutes.
5. Add toppings and serve.

Nutritional Information (Per Serving)
Calories: 177
Fat: 15 g
Sat Fat: 12.8 g
Carbohydrates: 10.4 g
Fiber: 2.5 g
Sugar: 2.1 g
Protein: 2.7 g
Sodium: 76 mg

Pumpkin Pie Sorghum

Serves: 6
Cooking Time: 25 minutes
Ingredients:
1½ cups sorghum, rinsed
1¼ cups pumpkin puree
1½ tablespoons pumpkin pie spice
1½ cups almond milk, unsweetened + extra to serve
3 tablespoons maple syrup
1½ teaspoons vanilla extract
3 cups water

Directions:
1. Add all the ingredients to the Instant Pot and stir.

2. Close the lid. Select MANUAL and cook at high pressure for 25 minutes.

3. When the cooking is complete, use a natural pressure release.

4. Serve with almond milk.

Nutritional Information (Per Serving)
Calories: 229
Fat: 2.6 g
Sat Fat: 0.4 g
Carbohydrates: 49.8 g
Fiber: 4.7 g
Sugar: 9.4 g
Protein: 6.3 g
Sodium: 42 mg

Instant Quinoa

Serves: 6
Cooking Time: 1 minutes
Ingredients:
2 cups quinoa, rinsed
2½ cups water
2 tablespoons maple syrup
½ teaspoon vanilla extract
⅓ teaspoon cinnamon
Dash of salt

Directions:

1. Add all of the ingredients to the Instant Pot. Stir thoroughly to combine.

2. Cook for 1 minute at high pressure.

3. When the cooking is complete, do a natural pressure release for 10 minutes. Quick release the remaining pressure.

4. Open the lid carefully. Serve quinoa with almond slivers and berries.

Nutritional Information (Per Serving)
Calories: 227
Fat: 3.4 g
Sat Fat: 0.4 g
Carbohydrates: 41 g
Fiber: 4 g
Sugar: 4 g
Protein: 8 g
Sodium: 43 mg

Mac and Cheese

Serves: 6
Cooking Time: 15 minutes
Ingredients:
2 cups whole wheat macaroni
1½ cans (14.5 ounces each) diced tomatoes, drained
⅓ cup vegan breadcrumbs + extra to sprinkle
1½ cups almond milk
1½ cups cashews, soaked in water overnight
⅓ cup water
2 tablespoons taco seasoning
3 teaspoons arrowroot flour
1½ teaspoons garlic powder
1½ teaspoons onion powder
¾ teaspoon paprika
½ teaspoon pepper powder
1 teaspoon salt

Directions:
1. Fill the Instant Pot with 3½ cups water and add the macaroni.
2. Cook for 4 minutes at high pressure. When the cooking is complete, do a quick pressure release.
3. Drain and leave the macaroni in the pot.
4. Add tomatoes and breadcrumbs into the pot.
5. Add rest of the ingredients into a blender and blend until smooth.
6. Pour into the Instant Pot and mix well.
7. Adjusted the SAUTÉ mode to SAUTÉ LESS. Bring to a boil and simmer for 5 minutes. Stir a couple of times while it is cooking.
8. Spoon into bowls. Sprinkle some breadcrumbs on top and serve.

Nutritional Information (Per Serving)
Calories: 395
Fat: 17.3 g
Sat Fat: 3.3 g
Carbohydrates: 52.4 g
Fiber: 5.6 g
Sugar: 7.4 g
Protein: 12.3 g
Sodium: 857 mg

Brown Rice

Serves: 4
Cooking Time: 24 minutes
Ingredients:
1½ cups brown rice, rinsed
1½ cups water
1 tablespoon olive oil
½ teaspoon salt

Directions:
1. Add all the ingredients to the Instant Pot and stir.

2. Close the lid. Select MANUAL and cook at high pressure for 24 minutes.

3. When the cooking is complete, let the pressure release naturally for 10 minutes. Quick release the remaining pressure.

4. Fluff with a fork and serve.

Nutritional Information (Per Serving)
Calories: 288
Fat: 5.4 g
Sat Fat: 0.9 g
Carbohydrates: 54.3 g
Fiber: 2.4 g
Sugar: 0 g
Protein: 5.3 g
Sodium: 294 mg

Vegan Buckwheat Porridge

Serves: 6
Cooking Time: 10 minutes
Ingredients:
1 cup buckwheat groats
3 cups coconut milk
2 cups water
1 large ripe banana, sliced
1 teaspoon cinnamon powder
1 teaspoon vanilla extract
3 tablespoons maple syrup
¼ cup raisins
1 cup grated coconut
Some chopped walnuts

Directions:
1. Rinse the buckwheat with water and drain. Add all the ingredients except the walnuts to the Instant Pot. Mix well.

2. Close the lid, choose MANUAL, and cook at high pressure for 10 minutes.

3. When the cooking is complete, do a natural pressure release.

4. Transfer the porridge into a large bowl.

5. Garnish with walnuts and serve.

Nutritional Information (Per Serving)
Calories: 457
Fat: 33.8 g
Sat Fat: 29.5 g
Carbohydrates: 39.6 g
Fiber: 6.7 g
Sugar: 17.8 g
Protein: 6.2 g
Sodium: 25 mg

Brown Rice & Green Tea Porridge

Serves: 6
Cooking Time: 30 minutes
Ingredients:
1 cup brown rice, rinsed
3 green tea bags
¼ cup lentils, rinsed
7 cups water
Salt to taste

Directions:

1. Add all the ingredients into the instant pot.

2. Close the lid, select MANUAL and cook at high pressure for 30 minutes.

3. When the cooking is complete, use a natural pressure release.

4. Discard tea bags. This porridge will not be very thick.

5. Serve warm.

Nutritional Information (Per Serving)
Calories: 121
Fat: 0.9 g
Sat Fat: 0.2 g
Carbohydrates: 25.3 g
Fiber: 1.3 g
Sugar: 0 g
Protein: 2.8 g

Multigrain Porridge

Serves: 6

Cooking Time: 20 minutes

Ingredients:

1 cup mixture of bulgur, oats, quinoa, millet, and buckwheat, or any other grains of your choice, soaked in water overnight, drained

1 cup coconut milk

4 cups water

Sweetener to taste (optional)

Directions:

1. Add all the ingredients into your Instant Pot.

2. Close the lid. Select the PORRIDGE button.

3. When the timer goes off, let the pressure release naturally.

4. Serve right away.

Nutritional Information (Per Serving)
Calories: 189
Fat: 10.5 g
Sat Fat: 8.7 g
Carbohydrates: 22.5 g
Fiber: 3.7 g
Sugar: 1.3 g
Protein: 4.7 g
Sodium: 11 mg

CHAPTER THREE

Vegan Instant Pot Recipes for Soups

Carrot and Sweet Potato Soup

Serves: 8
Cooking Time: 15 minutes
Ingredients:
6 large carrots, peeled and chopped
2 large celery stalks, chopped
2 cups sweet potatoes, peeled and chopped
4 stalks lemongrass, halved
4 cloves garlic, pressed
1-inch piece of ginger, minced
2 medium onions, chopped
2 cups coconut milk
4 cups vegetable broth
1 red chili, chopped
Salt to taste
Juice of a lime
Fresh cilantro leaves, chopped, to garnish
Sesame seeds to garnish

Directions:
1. Add all ingredients except lime juice to the Instant Pot.
2. Close the lid. Select the SOUP button and set the timer for 15 minutes.
3. When the timer goes off, do a quick pressure release. Discard lemongrass.
4. Cool for a while and blend with a hand blender. Add the lime juice while blending.
5. Ladle into bowls. Garnish with cilantro and sesame seeds.

6. Serve warm or cold.

Nutritional Information (Per Serving)
Calories: 246
Fat: 15.1 g
Sat Fat: 12.9 g
Carbohydrates: 25 g
Fiber: 5.1 g
Sugar: 7 g
Protein: 5.4 g

High Fiber Vegetable Soup

Serves: 6
Cooking Time: 5 minutes
Ingredients:
1 tablespoon vegetable oil
4 garlic cloves, minced
1 cup carrots, chopped
1 cup green bell pepper, chopped
1 cup shredded cabbage
1 cup broccoli florets
½ cup kidney beans
¼ cup quinoa
1 teaspoon oregano
1 tablespoon soy sauce
1 teaspoon onion powder
4 cups vegetable broth
¼ teaspoon salt
2 tablespoons lemon juice
Some ground pepper
Some basil leaves

Directions:
1. Set the Instant Pot to SAUTÉ and heat the vegetable oil.

2. Add minced garlic and sauté for about a minute.

3. Add remaining ingredients to the pot slowly, except for basil leaves and pepper. Stir to mix well.

4. Close the lid and cook at high pressure for 5 minutes.

5. Let the pressure release naturally, and transfer to large soup bowls.

6. Season with some ground pepper and garnish with basil leaves.

Nutritional Information (Per Serving)

Calories: 153
Fat: 4 g
Sat Fat: 0.8 g
Carbohydrates: 21 g
Fiber: 4.4 g
Sugar: 3.6 g
Protein: 9 g
Sodium: 780 mg

Wild Rice Soup

Serves: 8
Cooking Time: 40 minutes
Ingredients:
1½ cups onion, chopped
1 tablespoon olive oil
3 cloves garlic, minced
1½ cups carrots, chopped
1½ cups celery stalks, chopped
1½ cups dried chickpeas, soaked in water over night
2 bay leaves
1½ cups wild rice
1½ teaspoons dried thyme
7½ cups vegetable broth
1 cup water
¾ cup raw cashew, soaked in hot water for 30 minutes
Salt and pepper to taste

Directions:
1. Select SAUTÉ. Add oil and onions and sauté until translucent.
2. Stir in the garlic and sauté until fragrant. Stir in the carrots and celery and sauté for a couple of minutes.
3. Add chickpeas, bay leaf, wild rice, thyme, and broth. Press CANCEL.
4. Close the lid. Select MANUAL and cook at high pressure for 35 minutes.
5. When the timer goes off, let the pressure release naturally.
6. Add cashew and water into a blender and blend until smooth. Pour into the Instant Pot.
7. Add salt and pepper and mix well.
8. Ladle into soup bowls and serve.

Nutritional Information (Per Serving)

Calories: 396

Fat: 11.7 g

Sat Fat: 2.1 g

Carbohydrates: 56.5 g

Fiber: 10.4 g

Sugar: 8.8 g

Protein: 19 g

Creamy Broccoli Soup

Serves: 3
Cooking Time: 27 minutes
Ingredients:
6 tablespoons raw cashew, soaked in water for 3–4 hours
1 medium onion, chopped
2 medium carrots, chopped
7 ounces broccoli, chopped into florets
½ teaspoon salt
1 teaspoon olive oil
1 stalk celery, chopped
2 cloves garlic, minced
3 cups water, divided
Freshly ground pepper to taste

Directions:
1. Select SAUTÉ. Add oil. When the oil is heated, add onion and a pinch of salt and sauté until translucent.
2. Stir in the carrots and celery and sauté for 2–3 minutes.
3. Add garlic and broccoli and sauté for a couple of minutes.
4. Add 2½ cups water. Add salt and pepper. Press CANCEL.
5. Close the lid. Select the SOUP button and set the timer for 20 minutes.
6. When the timer goes off, let the pressure release naturally.
7. When the soup is cool enough to handle, blend it in a blender until smooth. Transfer to a bowl.
8. Add cashew into the blender with ½ cup water and blend until smooth. Pour into the soup. Stir well. Heat if desired.
9. Taste, adjust the seasoning and serve.

Nutritional Information (Per Serving)
Calories: 170
Fat: 9.8 g
Sat Fat: 1.8 g
Carbohydrates: 18.3 g
Fiber: 4.2 g
Sugar: 5.6 g
Protein: 5.4 g
Sodium: 454 mg

Chard, Lentil and Potato Soup

Serves: 4
Cooking Time: 35 minutes
Ingredients:
1½ tablespoons olive oil
1 medium onion, chopped
1 medium carrot, sliced
1 small stalk celery, chopped
2 cups Swiss chard, chopped
2 medium Yukon gold potatoes, cubed
½ tablespoon soy sauce
1 clove garlic, minced
1½ cups lentils, rinsed
3 cups vegetable broth
Salt and pepper to taste

Directions:
1. Select the SAUTÉ button. Add oil. When the oil is heated, add onion, garlic, stems of Swiss chard and celery and sauté until translucent. Press the CANCEL button.

2. Add rest of the ingredients except the Swiss chard leaves and stir.

3. Close the lid. Select SOUP and use the default setting.

4. When the timer goes off, let the pressure release naturally.

5. Add Swiss chard leaves. Press SAUTÉ and simmer until Swiss chard wilts.

6. Ladle into soup bowls and serve.

Nutritional Information (Per Serving)
Calories: 408
Fat: 8 g
Sat Fat: 1.3 g
Carbohydrates: 63.4 g

Fiber: 10.2 g
Sugar: 3.2 g
Protein: 24.2 g

Butternut Squash Soup

Serves: 8
Cooking Time: 30 minutes
Ingredients:
6 cups butternut squash, peeled and diced
1 large onion, chopped
3 large carrots, chopped
2 cups celery stalk, chopped
4 garlic cloves, minced
6 cups vegetable broth
1 teaspoon cayenne pepper
¼ teaspoon salt
1½ cups coconut milk
2 teaspoons dried oregano
1 teaspoon paprika
Some parsley leaves

Directions:
1. Set the Instant Pot to SAUTÉ. Add the butternut squash, chopped onion, carrots, garlic, and celery.

2. Pour in the broth, and bring this mixture to a boil.

3. Press CANCEL. Close the lid and select SOUP and the default setting.

4. When the cooking is complete, do a natural pressure release.

5. Open the lid and let the mixture cool down.

6. Using a hand blender, blend all ingredients into a fine paste.

7. Set the Instant Pot to SAUTÉ. Add oregano, coconut milk, cayenne pepper, paprika, and salt. Let it simmer for 5 minutes.

8. Garnish with fresh parsley and serve.

Nutritional Information (Per Serving)

Calories: 207
Fat: 12.1 g
Sat Fat: 9.9 g
Carbohydrates: 21.6 g
Fiber: 4.9 g
Sugar: 6.9 g
Protein: 6.5 g
Sodium: 697 mg

Corn and Red Pepper Chowder

Serves: 4
Cooking Time: 35 minutes
Ingredients:
2 tablespoons olive oil
1 medium red bell peppers, chopped + extra to garnish
4 cups frozen corn kernels, divided
1 medium yellow onions, chopped
3 medium Yukon gold potatoes, chopped
4 cups vegetable broth
½ teaspoon smoked paprika
1 teaspoon ground cumin
⅛ teaspoon cayenne pepper
1 cup almond milk
Freshly ground pepper to taste
1 scallion, chopped, to garnish

Directions:
1. Select SAUTÉ. Add oil. When the oil is heated, add onion and sauté until translucent.
2. Add red bell pepper, 1 cup corn, potatoes, broth, salt, and spices. Press CANCEL.
3. Close the lid. Select MANUAL and cook at high pressure for 15 minutes.
4. When the timer goes off, let the pressure release naturally. Cool for a while.
5. Blend in a blender until smooth. Add it back into the pot.
6. Add the remaining corn and almond milk.
7. Press SAUTÉ and simmer for 15 minutes.
8. Add salt and pepper to taste and mix well.
9. Ladle into soup bowls. Garnish with scallions and red bell pepper and serve.

Nutritional Information (Per Serving)
Calories: 366
Fat: 10.5 g
Sat Fat: 1.6 g
Carbohydrates: 62.6 g
Fiber: 6.9 g
Sugar: 10.8 g
Protein: 12.7 g
Sodium: 590 mg

Vegan Lasagna Soup

Serves: 4
Cooking Time: 20 minutes
Ingredients:
For lasagna:
2½ cups vegetable broth
2 cloves garlic, minced
1 small onion, chopped
6 tablespoons lentils, rinsed
7 ounces canned diced tomatoes
7 ounces canned crushed tomatoes
½ teaspoon dried oregano
½ teaspoon dried basil
1½ cups spinach, chopped
4 lasagna noodles, broken into pieces
Salt and pepper to taste

For vegan ricotta cheese:
½ cup raw cashews, soaked in water for 4–5 hours, rinsed and drained
2 ounces extra firm tofu, drained
½ tablespoon lemon juice
2 tablespoons almond milk
2 tablespoons vegan pesto
Salt and pepper to taste

Directions:
1. For lasagna, add all the ingredients into the Instant Pot and stir.
2. Close the lid. Select MANUAL and cook at high pressure for 20 minutes.
3. When the cooking is complete, do a natural pressure release for 10 minutes. Quick release the remaining pressure.

4. Meanwhile, make the vegan ricotta cheese as follows: Blend together cashew and almond milk in a blender until smooth. Add tofu and pulse until well combined and smooth. Add rest of the ingredients of ricotta and pulse.

5. Ladle into soup bowls and serve topped with the vegan ricotta cheese.

Nutritional Information (Per Serving)
Calories: 436
Fat: 13.8 g
Sat Fat: 3.9 g
Carbohydrates: 62.4 g
Fiber: 9.7 g
Sugar: 7.2 g
Protein: 19.2 g

Coconut Chickpea Curry

Serves: 4
Cooking Time: 30 minutes
Ingredients:
1 can (15 ounces) chickpeas, rinsed and drained
1 medium sweet potato, cubed
1 tablespoon curry powder
½ teaspoon ginger, minced
½ teaspoon ground turmeric
3 cups vegetable broth
½ cup dry lentils, rinsed
1 cup coconut milk
Salt and pepper to taste

Directions:
1. Add all the ingredients into the Instant Pot.

2. Close the lid. Select BEAN/CHILI and use the default setting.

3. When the timer goes off, let the pressure release naturally.

4. Ladle into soup bowls and serve.

Nutritional Information (Per Serving)
Calories: 421
Fat: 18.2 g
Sat Fat: 13.3 g
Carbohydrates: 48.3 g
Fiber: 16.7 g
Sugar: 8.9 g
Protein: 19.3 g

Hot and Sour Soup

Serves: 6
Cooking Time: 10 minutes
Ingredients:
6 cloves garlic, minced
3 tablespoons ginger, grated, divided
12 shiitake mushrooms, stemmed and sliced
15 ounces mushrooms, sliced
1½ packages (15 ounces each) silken tofu, chopped into small cubes
1½ cans (8 ounces each) bamboo shoots, drained, julienned
2 cups frozen green peas
6 cups water
1½ teaspoons chili paste
3 tablespoons soy sauce
3 tablespoons vinegar
1½ teaspoons sesame oil
Salt and pepper to taste

Directions:
1. Add all the ingredients except half the ginger to the Instant Pot.
2. Close the lid. Select MANUAL and cook at high pressure for 10 minutes.
3. When the cooking is complete, use a natural pressure release.
4. Add remaining ginger and stir.
5. Ladle into soup bowls and serve.

Nutritional Information (Per Serving)
Calories: 231
Fat: 5.1 g
Sat Fat: 0.8 g

Carbohydrates: 35.8 g
Fiber: 6.9 g
Sugar: 11.4 g
Protein: 16 g

Split Pea Soup

Serves: 4
Cooking Time: 30 minutes
Ingredients:
1 cup split peas, rinsed
1 potato, cubed
1 carrot, sliced
1 clove garlic, minced
1 medium onion, chopped
1 celery stalk, chopped
4 cups vegetable broth
½ teaspoon ground cumin
½ teaspoon dry mustard
½ teaspoon sage
2 bay leaves
½ teaspoon dried thyme

Directions:
1. Add all the ingredients into the Instant Pot and stir to mix.
2. Close the lid. Select BEAM/CHILI and use the default setting.
3. When the timer goes off, let the pressure release naturally.
4. Discard the bay leaves. Ladle into soup bowls and serve.

Nutritional Information (Per Serving)

Calories: 263
Fat: 2.2 g
Sat Fat: 0.5 g
Carbohydrates: 43.1 g
Fiber: 14.8 g
Sugar: 7.1 g
Protein: 18.5 g
Sodium: 793 mg

Vegetarian Minestrone Soup

Serves: 8
Cooking Time: 8 minutes
Ingredients:
8 cups vegetable broth
4 bay leaves
8 large tomatoes, chopped
6 carrots, chopped
6 stalks celery, chopped
3 yellow crookneck squashes, chopped
1 large onion, diced
4 small zucchinis, chopped
2 cups green beans
6 cloves garlic, minced
3 cups pasta, uncooked
Salt and pepper to taste

Directions:
1. Add all the ingredients into the Instant Pot.
2. Close the lid. Select MANUAL and cook at high pressure for 8 minutes.
3. During the last 15 minutes of cooking, add pasta.
4. When the cooking is complete, carefully do a quick pressure release.

5. Discard the bay leaves. Ladle into soup bowls and serve.

Nutritional Information (Per Serving)
Calories: 271
Fat: 2.9 g
Sat Fat: 0.6 g
Carbohydrates: 52.6 g
Fiber: 10.5 g
Sugar: 11.2 g
Protein: 12.2 g
Sodium: 821 mg

CHAPTER FOUR

Instant Pot Recipes for Vegetables

Garlicky Bell Peppers

Serves: 4
Cooking Time: 5 minutes
Ingredients:
2 tablespoons olive oil
8 garlic cloves, minced
2 jalapeño peppers, seeded and chopped
2 green bell peppers, seeded and cut into long strips
2 red bell peppers, seeded and cut into long strips
2 yellow bell peppers, seeded and cut into long strips
2 orange bell pepper, seeded and cut into long strips
Salt and pepper to taste
¾ cup water
2 tablespoons fresh lemon juice

Directions:
1. Place the oil in the Instant Pot and select SAUTÉ. Add the garlic and jalapeño and cook for 1 minute.
2. Press CANCEL and stir in remaining ingredients, except lemon juice.
3. Secure the lid and cook at high pressure for 2 minutes.
4. When the cooking is complete, use a quick pressure release.
5. Remove the lid and select SAUTÉ.
6. Stir in lemon juice and cook for 1–2 minutes.
7. Press CANCEL and serve.

Nutritional Information (Per Serving)
Calories: 121

Fat: 7.6 g
Sat Fat: 1.2 g
Carbohydrates: 13.7 g
Fiber: 4.5 g
Sugar: 6.2 g
Protein: 2.6 g

Vegetable Mélange

Serves: 3
Cooking Time: 10 minutes
Ingredients:
2 tablespoons olive oil
1 medium onion, chopped
1 small bell pepper, sliced
2 stalks celery, sliced
1 clove garlic, chopped
2 tomatoes, deseeded and chopped
4 potatoes, cut into ½ inch slices
1 zucchini, chopped into chunks
1 large carrot, cut into ½ inch slices
1 cup vegetable broth
2 tablespoons fresh dill, chopped
2 tablespoons parsley, chopped
½ cup frozen peas
Salt and pepper to taste

Directions:
1. Set the Instant Pot to SAUTÉ. Add oil. When oil is heated, add onions, bell pepper, celery, and garlic and sauté until onions are translucent. Press CANCEL.

2. Add rest of the ingredients.

3. Close the lid. Select MANUAL and cook at high pressure for 5 minutes.

4. When the timer goes off, let the pressure release naturally for 5 minutes. Quick release the remaining pressure.

5. Drain extra liquid and serve.

Nutritional Information (Per Serving)
Calories: 381
Fat: 10.7 g

Sat Fat: 1.6 g
Carbohydrates: 64.9 g
Fiber: 12.5 g
Sugar: 12.9 g
Protein: 10.9 g

Eggplant Italiano

Serves: 8
Cooking Time: 4 minutes
Ingredients:
2½ pounds eggplant, cut into 1-inch cubes
4 celery stalks, cut into 1-inch pieces
2 large onions, thinly sliced
7½ ounces canned tomato sauce
2 cans (16 ounce each) diced tomatoes with its juice
2 tablespoons olive oil, divided
1 cup olives, pitted and halved
4 tablespoons balsamic vinegar
2 tablespoons capers, drained
1 tablespoon maple syrup
2 teaspoon dried basil
Salt and pepper to taste
Basil leaves to garnish

Directions:
1. Add all the ingredients into the Instant Pot. Stir to mix well.

2. Close the lid. Select MANUAL and cook at high pressure for 4 minutes.

3. When the cooking is complete, do a quick pressure release.

4. Garnish with fresh basil and serve over rice or egg noodles.

Nutritional Information (Per Serving)
Calories: 127
Fat: 5.8 g
Sat Fat: 0.8 g
Carbohydrates: 18.5 g
Fiber: 6.9 g
Sugar: 10.4 g

Protein: 3 g

Veg Chow Mein

Serves: 6
Cooking Time: 10 minutes
Ingredients:
1½ pounds vegetarian chicken, chopped
4 medium carrots, chopped
2½ cup celery stalks, chopped
9 scallions, sliced
1½ cups bean sprouts
1½ cans (8 ounce each) water chestnuts, sliced
¾ teaspoon ginger, minced
1½ cups vegetable broth
3 tablespoons soy sauce
½ teaspoon red pepper flakes
Salt to taste
6 tablespoons corn starch mixed with 2/3 cup water

Directions:
1. Add all the ingredients except cornstarch mixture to the Instant Pot.
2. Close the lid, select MANUAL and cook at high pressure for 4 minutes.
3. When the cooking is complete, press CANCEL, do a quick pressure release.
4. Combine the cornstarch with water in a bowl and whisk. Pour this mixture into the pot, stirring continuously. Set the Instant Pot to SAUTÉ. Bring it to a boil until it thickens.
5. Serve hot over rice.

Nutritional Information (Per Serving)

Calories: 331
Fat: 3 g
Sat Fat: 0.2 g
Carbohydrates: 52.6 g
Fiber: 5.4 g
Sugar: 4.4 g
Protein: 18 g

Spiced Okra

Serves: 4
Cooking Time: 8 minutes
Ingredients:
2 tablespoons olive oil
6 garlic cloves, chopped
1 teaspoon cumin seeds
2 medium onions, sliced
2 medium tomatoes, chopped
2 pounds okra, cut into 1-inch pieces
½ cup vegetable broth
1 teaspoon ground coriander
½ teaspoon red chili powder
½ teaspoon ground turmeric
Salt and pepper to taste

Directions:
1. Place the oil in the Instant Pot and select SAUTÉ. Add the garlic and cumin seeds and cook for 1 minute.
2. Add the onion and cook for 4 minutes.
3. Add the remaining ingredients and cook for 1 more minute.
4. Press CANCEL and stir well.
5. Secure the lid and cook at high pressure for 2 minutes.
6. When the cooking is complete, do a quick pressure release.

7. Serve hot.

Nutritional Information (Per Serving)
Calories: 199
Fat: 8 g
Sat Fat: 1.2 g
Carbohydrates: 26.6 g
Fiber: 9.5 g
Sugar: 7.5 g
Protein: 6.6 g

Spinach with Tomatoes

Serves: 4
Cooking Time: 12 minutes
Ingredients:
2 tablespoons olive oil
2 small onions, chopped
2 teaspoons garlic, minced
10 cups fresh spinach, chopped
1 cup tomatoes, chopped
½ cup tomato puree
1½ cups vegetable broth
1 tablespoon fresh lemon juice
½ teaspoon red pepper flakes, crushed
Salt and pepper to taste

Directions:
1. Place the oil in the Instant Pot and select SAUTÉ. Add the onion and cook for about 3 minutes.
2. Add the garlic and red pepper flakes and cook for 1 minute.
3. Add spinach and cook for 2 minutes.
4. Press the CANCEL button and stir in the remaining ingredients.

5. Secure the lid and cook at high pressure for 6 minutes.

6. When the cooking is complete, carefully do a quick pressure release.

7. Serve warm.

Nutritional Information (Per Serving)
Calories: 168
Fat: 9.5 g
Sat Fat: 1.6 g
Carbohydrates: 12.5 g
Fiber: 3.6 g
Sugar: 5.6 g
Protein: 10.3 g

Quinoa with Mushrooms and Peppers

Serves: 8
Cooking Time: 15 minutes
Ingredients:
2½ cups quinoa, rinsed
2 onions, chopped
20 medium button mushrooms, diced
1 red chili, minced
2 medium red bell peppers, sliced
2 medium green bell peppers, sliced
4 tablespoons miso paste
4 tablespoons soy sauce
2½ cups vegetable broth
6 tablespoons olive oil
Salt to taste
4 cloves garlic, grated, finely chopped
2 tablespoons tomato paste
2 tablespoons lemon juice
A handful fresh cilantro, chopped to serve

Directions:

1. Press the SAUTÉ button. Add oil. When the oil is heated, add onion, mushroom, salt and chili and sauté until onion turns translucent.

2. Add the quinoa along with the remaining ingredients and stir. Press CANCEL.

3. Close the lid. Select MANUAL and cook at high pressure for 5 minutes.

4. When the cooking is complete, do a natural pressure release for 10 minutes. Quick release the remaining pressure.

5. Fluff with a fork and serve.

Nutritional Information (Per Serving)
Calories: 348

Fat: 14.5 g
Sat Fat: 2 g
Carbohydrates: 45.7 g
Fiber: 6.5 g
Sugar: 4.9 g
Protein: 11.5 g

Vegetable Curry with Tofu

Serves: 8
Cooking Time: 14 minutes
Ingredients:
32 ounces extra firm tofu, drained
1 tablespoon olive oil
2 cups eggplants, chopped
1 large onion, chopped
1½ cups frozen peas
1 large green bell pepper, sliced
1 large red bell pepper, sliced
2 tablespoons fresh ginger, minced
6 tablespoons Thai green or red curry paste
2 cans (14.5 ounces each) coconut milk
2 tablespoons coconut sugar or to taste
¾ cup vegetable broth
1 teaspoon turmeric powder
Salt to taste

Directions:
1. To press tofu, place something heavy over the tofu for at least 30 minutes and after that place over layers of paper towels. Chop into bite sized pieces.
2. Set the Instant Pot to SAUTÉ. Add oil and tofu and cook until golden brown. Press CANCEL and set the tofu aside.
3. Add the rest ingredients to the pot and mix.
4. Close the lid. Select MANUAL and cook at high pressure for 4 minutes.
5. When the cooking is complete, do a quick pressure release.
6. Open the lid, add tofu, and stir.
7. Serve hot over cooked quinoa or brown rice.

Nutritional Information (Per Serving)
Calories: 441
Fat: 36 g
Sat Fat: 25.3 g
Carbohydrates: 21.5 g
Fiber: 6.3 g
Sugar: 10.7 g
Protein: 13.9 g

Vegetable Succotash

Serves: 8
Cooking Time: 4 minutes
Ingredients:
4 cups zucchini, diced
4 cups corn kernels
1 cup onion, diced
2 cups okra, sliced
6 cloves garlic, minced
2 cans (10 ounces each) diced tomatoes in juice
1 cup vegetable broth
Salt and pepper to taste
½ teaspoon red pepper flakes
4 tablespoons lemon juice
1 teaspoon hot sauce
2 tablespoons fresh parsley, chopped

Directions:
1. Add tomatoes with juice, broth, corn, okra, zucchini, onions, garlic, salt, pepper, and red pepper flakes into the Instant Pot and mix well.

2. Close the lid. Select MANUAL and cook at high pressure for 4 minutes.

3. When the cooking is complete, do a quick pressure release.

4. Open the lid, add parsley, lemon juice and hot sauce and mix well.

5. Serve hot as it is in bowls or over rice.

Nutritional Information (Per Serving)
Calories: 114
Fat: 1.5 g
Sat Fat: 0.3 g
Carbohydrates: 23.5 g

Fiber: 4.8 g
Sugar: 6.6 g
Protein: 5.3 g

Cabbage with Carrot

Serves: 4
Cooking Time: 10 minutes
Ingredients:
2 tablespoons coconut oil
2 small onions, sliced
Salt to taste
2 garlic cloves, chopped
1 jalapeño pepper, seeded and chopped
1 tablespoon mild curry powder
1 medium head cabbage, shredded
2 small carrots, peeled and sliced
½ cup desiccated unsweetened coconut
2 tablespoons fresh lemon juice
1 cup water

Directions:
1. Place the coconut oil in the Instant Pot and select SAUTÉ. Add the onion and salt and cook for 4 minutes.

2. Add the garlic, jalapeño and curry powder and cook for 1 minute.

3. Press CANCEL and stir in remaining ingredients.

4. Secure the lid and cook at high pressure for 5 minutes.

5. When the cooking is complete, do a natural pressure release for 5 minutes. Quick release the remaining pressure.

6. Serve warm.

Nutritional Information (Per Serving)
Calories: 192
Fat: 10 g
Sat Fat: 8.5 g
Carbohydrates: 25.5 g
Fiber: 8.6 g
Sugar: 13.7 g
Protein: 4.2 g

Cauliflower Bolognese with Zucchini Noodles

Serves: 2
Cooking Time: 3 minutes
Ingredients:
1 medium head cauliflower, broken into florets
2 cloves garlic, minced
½ cup onions, diced
¾ teaspoon dried basil
Red pepper flakes to taste
1 teaspoon dried oregano flakes
¼ cup vegetable broth
1½ cans (14 ounce each) diced tomatoes, without salt
Salt and pepper to taste

For the noodles:
4 medium zucchinis

Directions:
1. Add all the ingredients except zucchini to the Instant Pot.
2. Close the lid. Select MANUAL and cook at high pressure for 3 minutes.
3. When the cooking is complete, do a quick pressure release.
4. Meanwhile make noodles of the zucchini using a spiralizer using blade A or a julienne peeler.
5. Mash the cauliflower with a potato masher or in a food processor.
6. Divide the noodles in 4 bowls. Place cauliflower Bolognese over it and serve.

Nutritional Information (Per Serving)
Calories: 211

Fat: 1.9 g
Sat Fat: 0.3 g
Carbohydrates: 44.2 g
Fiber: 16.1 g
Sugar: 22.9 g
Protein: 14.3 g

Barbecued Tofu and Vegetables

Serves: 6
Cooking Time: 15 minutes
Ingredients:
1½ packages (16 ounces each) extra firm tofu, press to remove excess moisture, chopped into ½ inch thick pieces
1 tablespoon olive oil

For sauce:
3 teaspoons fresh ginger, minced
5 cloves garlic, minced
1 large onion, minced
½ teaspoon vegan Worcestershire sauce
12 ounces tomato sauce, unsalted
1½ tablespoons low sodium soy sauce
3 tablespoons rice wine vinegar
1½ tablespoons spicy brown mustard
3 teaspoons molasses
½ teaspoon crushed red pepper
½ teaspoon five spice powder
Salt to taste
3 tablespoons water

For vegetables:
3 medium zucchinis, chopped into ½-inch cubes
4 stalks broccoli (use only stalks), chop into ¼ inch thick slices
1½ cans (8 ounces each) water chestnuts, sliced
1 medium red bell pepper, chopped into 1-inch squares
1 medium green bell pepper, chopped into 1-inch squares

Directions:
1. Heat the oil in a nonstick skillet over medium heat. Add tofu and cook until brown on both the sides. Set aside.

2. Set the Instant Pot to SAUTÉ and spray the pot with cooking spray. Add onion, ginger, and garlic and sauté until onions are translucent.

3. Add tofu and remaining ingredients of the sauce and stir. Press CANCEL.

4. Close the lid, select MANUAL, and cook at high pressure for 4 minutes.

5. When the cooking is complete, do a quick pressure release.

6. Open the lid, add the vegetables, and mix well.

7. Close the lid, select MANUAL, and cook at high pressure for 3 more minutes.

8. When the cooking is complete, do a quick pressure release.

9. Serve hot over brown rice.

Nutritional Information (Per Serving)
Calories: 280
Fat: 7.9 g
Sat Fat: 1.4 g
Carbohydrates: 40.2 g
Fiber: 4.8 g
Sugar: 10.4 g
Protein: 14.7 g

Green Bean Warm Salad

Serves: 3
Cooking Time: 12 minutes
Ingredients:
For the salad:
½ ounce dry porcini mushrooms
1 pound potatoes, peeled, cut into 1-inch chunks
1 pound fresh green beans, trimmed and cut into 2-inch pieces
½ teaspoon salt, divided
1 cup boiling water

Directions:
1. Place mushrooms in a bowl. Pour boiling water over it. Cover and set aside for 5 minutes.

2. Add mushrooms along with the water into the Instant Pot. Place potatoes over it. Sprinkle with half the salt.

3. Place a steamer basket over the potatoes and place green beans on the steamer basket. Sprinkle the remaining salt over it.

4. Close the lid. Select MANUAL and cook at high pressure for 5 minutes.

5. When the cooking is complete, do a natural pressure release for 5 minutes. Quick release the remaining pressure.

6. Transfer the beans, potatoes, and mushrooms along with the cooked liquid into a serving bowl. Toss well.

7. Add your favorite seasonings and serve.

Nutritional Information (Per Serving)
Calories: 169
Fat: 0.3 g
Sat Fat: 0.1 g
Carbohydrates: 36.9 g
Fiber: 10 g
Sugar: 3.9 g

Protein: 6.5 g
Sodium: 406 mg

Beets and Garlic Sauté

Serves: 6
Cooking Time: 15 minutes
Ingredients:
6 medium beets, trimmed
1 teaspoon salt
2 tablespoons olive oil
2 teaspoons lemon juice
4 cloves garlic, minced

Directions:

1. Arrange a trivet in the Instant Pot. Add 1 cup of water in the Instant Pot.

2. Place the beets on top of trivet in a single layer.

3. Close the lid, select MANUAL, and cook at high pressure for 20 minutes.

4. When the cooking is complete, do a quick pressure release.

5. Remove the beets with tongs and place on your cutting board. When cool enough to handle, chop into pieces.

6. Place a skillet over medium high heat. Add oil. When the oil is heated, add beets. Stir only after 3 minutes. Add garlic and sauté until tender.

7. Sprinkle with lemon juice and toss well.

8. Serve hot.

Nutritional Information (Per Serving)
Calories: 87
Fat: 4.9 g
Sat Fat: 0.7 g
Carbohydrates: 10.7 g
Fiber: 2.1 g
Sugar: 8 g
Protein: 1.8 g
Sodium: 465 mg

Tangy Sweet Potato Wedges

Serves: 4
Cooking Time: 20 minutes
Ingredients:
3 large sweet potatoes
½ teaspoon salt
1 tablespoon dry mango powder
1 teaspoon paprika
2 tablespoons vegetable oil
1 cup water

Directions:
1. Wash the sweet potatoes thoroughly and peel them. Cut into medium-sized wedges.
2. Add 1 cup water and place a trivet in the Instant Pot.
3. Lay the sweet potato wedges on it and cook for 15 minutes at high pressure.
4. When the cooking is complete, do a quick pressure release.
5. Remove and place the wedges on a plate.
6. Heat the vegetable oil in a saucepan over medium-high heat. Slide in the sweet potato wedges and pan sear until they turn brown.
7. Combine dry mango powder, salt, and paprika in a bowl and mix well.
8. Coat the wedges generously with this mixture and serve.

Nutritional Information (Per Serving)
Calories: 196
Fat: 7.1 g
Sat Fat: 1.4 g
Carbohydrates: 32.1 g
Fiber: 4.9 g
Sugar: 1 g

Protein: 1.8 g
Sodium: 10 mg

CHAPTER FIVE

Vegan Instant Pot Recipes for Desserts

Pumpkin Date Pudding

Serves: 12
Cooking Time: 30 minutes
Ingredients:

2 cups short grain brown rice, soaked in water for a couple of hours

1 cup dates, pitted and diced

6 cups coconut milk

1 cup water

2 sticks cinnamon

¼ teaspoon salt

2 teaspoons pumpkin pie spice mix + extra to garnish

2 cups pumpkin puree

2 teaspoons vanilla extract

1 cup maple syrup

Directions:

1. Add coconut milk, water, rice, dates, salt, and cinnamon into the Instant Pot.

2. Close the lid, select MANUAL, and cook at high pressure for 20 minutes.

3. When the cooking is complete, use a natural pressure release.

4. Stir in the remaining ingredients.

5. Set the Instant Pot to SAUTÉ. Let it simmer for a few minutes, stirring constantly. Discard the cinnamon sticks.

6. Spoon into bowls. Sprinkle pumpkin spice on top.

7. Serve warm or cold.

Nutritional Information (Per Serving)
Calories: 431
Fat: 29.1 g
Sat Fat: 25.4 g
Carbohydrates: 45.2 g
Fiber: 5.5 g
Sugar: 30.6 g
Protein: 4.1 g
Sodium: 23 mg

Chai Spiced Pears

Serves: 6
Cooking Time: 8 minutes
Ingredients:
6 ripe, medium sized pears, peeled and cored
2 sticks cinnamon
7 pods cardamom
3 cups orange juice
1 teaspoon fresh ginger, minced
6 tablespoons maple syrup
1 teaspoon ground cinnamon
¼ cup walnuts, roughly chopped

Directions:

1. Add all the ingredients except walnuts and ground cinnamon to the Instant Pot.

2. Close the lid, select MANUAL, and cook at high pressure for 8 minutes.

3. When the cooking is complete, use a natural pressure release. Discard the cinnamon sticks.

4. Sprinkle with cinnamon and walnuts and serve warm.

Nutritional Information (Per Serving)
Calories: 212
Fat: 3.8 g
Sat Fat: 0.3 g
Carbohydrates: 45.2 g
Fiber: 6.3 g
Sugar: 29 g
Protein: 2.5 g
Sodium: 6 mg

Coconut Rice Pudding

Serves: 10
Cooking Time: 20 minutes
Ingredients:
¾ cup short grain white rice, rinsed
½ cup maple syrup
½ cup shredded coconut
½ teaspoon kosher salt
4 cups coconut milk
3 cups vanilla flavored coconut milk, unsweetened
¼ cup toasted coconut, to garnish
1 teaspoon vanilla extract

Directions:

1. Add rice, map syrup, shredded coconut, salt, 3 cups coconut milk and 2 cups vanilla coconut milk into the Instant Pot. Mix well.

2. Close the lid, select MANUAL, and cook at high pressure for 20 minutes.

3. When the cooking is complete, use a natural pressure release.

4. Open the lid, add the remaining coconut milk and vanilla extract, and mix well.

5. Transfer into serving bowls. Cool for 15 minutes.

6. Serve warm topped with toasted coconut.

Nutritional Information (Per Serving)
Calories: 501
Fat: 42.2 g
Sat Fat: 37.3 g
Carbohydrates: 32.1 g
Fiber: 4.4 g
Sugar: 15.4 g
Protein: 5.1 g
Sodium: 29 mg

Pear and Cranberry Cake

Serves: 8
Cooking Time: 45 minutes
Ingredients:
For dry ingredients:
2½ cups whole wheat flour
1 teaspoon baking powder
1 teaspoon baking soda
¼ teaspoon salt
1 teaspoon ground cardamom

For wet ingredients:
1 cup coconut milk
4 tablespoons ground flaxseeds
½ cup agave nectar
4 tablespoons apple sauce

Other ingredients:
1 cup fresh cranberries
2 cups pears, chopped

Directions:
1. Grease a Bundt pan that fits inside the Instant Pot with a little oil.
2. Add all the dry ingredients to a bowl and mix well.
3. Add all the wet ingredients to another bowl and mix well.
4. Pour the wet ingredients into the bowl of dry ingredients and mix well.
5. Add pears and cranberries and mix well. Pour the batter into the prepared pan.
6. Cover the pan with foil.
7. Place a steamer rack inside the instant pot. Pour 3 cups water in it. Place the pan over the rack.

8. Close the lid, select MANUAL, and cook at high pressure for 45 minutes.

9. When the timer goes off, let the pressure release naturally.

10. Remove the pan from the pot and uncover. Let it cool completely.

11. Slice and serve.

Nutritional Information (Per Serving)
Calories: 323
Fat: 8.7 g
Sat Fat: 6.6 g
Carbohydrates: 55.7 g
Fiber: 4.5 g
Sugar: 20.9 g
Protein: 5.6 g
Sodium: 240 mg

Apple Crumble

Serves: 8
Cooking Time: 10 minutes
Ingredients:
8 apples, sliced
1 cup water
1 teaspoon ground cinnamon
½ teaspoon ground nutmeg
4 tablespoons vegan margarine
4 tablespoons maple syrup
4 cups granola

Directions:

1. Lay the apple slices in the Instant Pot. Add water, maple syrup, spices, and margarine. Mix well.

2. Top with granola.

3. Close the lid. Select MANUAL and cook at high pressure for 10 minutes.

4. When the cooking is complete, use a natural pressure release.

5. Serve warm.

Nutritional Information (Per Serving)
Calories: 247
Fat: 7 g
Sat Fat: 1 g
Carbohydrates: 46.8 g
Fiber: 7.1 g
Sugar: 25.3 g
Protein: 3.1 g
Sodium: 71 mg

Buckwheat Pudding

Serves: 8
Cooking Time: 8 minutes
Ingredients:
2 cups buckwheat groats, rinsed
2 bananas, sliced
2 teaspoons ground cinnamon
6 cups rice milk
1 teaspoon vanilla extract
½ cup raisins
Chopped nuts to garnish

Directions:
1. Add all the ingredients into the Instant Pot and stir.
2. Close the lid, select MANUAL, and cook at high pressure for 8 minutes.
3. When the timer goes off, let the pressure release naturally.
4. Spoon into bowls. Cool slightly. Garnish with nuts and serve.

Nutritional Information (Per Serving)
Calories: 247
Fat: 2.6 g
Sat Fat: 0.4 g
Carbohydrates: 54.3 g
Fiber: 4.4 g
Sugar: 9.8 g
Protein: 4.7 g
Sodium: 69 mg

Cranberry Stuffed Apples

Serves: 6
Cooking Time: 10 minutes
Ingredients:
6 medium apples
½ cup walnuts, chopped
4 tablespoons maple syrup
½ cup cranberries
¼ teaspoon ground nutmeg
½ teaspoon ground cinnamon
1 cup water
Some cashews, roasted and chopped

Directions:
1. Leave the bottom part of the apples as it is and core the apples. Slowly scoop out some more pulp from inside the apple.

2. In a bowl, mix together rest of the ingredients except the cashews, and fill inside the apple.

3. Add water to the Instant Pot. Add the apples to the pot, so that they are standing.

4. Close the lid, select MANUAL, and cook at high pressure for 10 minutes.

5. When the cooking is complete, use a natural pressure release.

6. Sprinkle with cashews and serve hot.

Nutritional Information (Per Serving)
Calories: 221
Fat: 6.6 g
Sat Fat: 0.4 g
Carbohydrates: 41.8 g
Fiber: 6.6 g
Sugar: 31.6 g
Protein: 3.1 g

Sodium: 3 mg

Tapioca Pudding

Serves: 6
Cooking Time: 15 minutes
Ingredients:
½ cup tapioca pearls, soaked for at least 1 hour
1 cups coconut milk
½ cup maple syrup
Some lemon zest
3 tablespoons chopped cashews
6 roasted cashews for garnishing

Directions:
1. Add the soaked tapioca pearls, coconut milk, maple syrup, chopped cashews, and lemon zest to an Instant Pot. Mix well.

2. Close the lid, select MANUAL, and cook at high pressure for 10 minutes.

3. When the cooking is complete, do a natural pressure release.

4. Serve chilled with roasted cashews on top.

Nutritional Information (Per Serving)
Calories: 239
Fat: 12.3 g
Sat Fat: 9 g
Carbohydrates: 32.9 g
Fiber: 1.2 g
Sugar: 17.7 g
Protein: 1.8 g
Sodium: 9 mg

Fresh Berry Compote

Serves: 8
Cooking Time: 2 minutes
Ingredients:
4 cups blueberries
4 cups strawberries, halved
4 tablespoons lemon juice
4 tablespoons maple syrup

Directions:
1. Add strawberries, maple syrup, lemon juice and ⅓ of the blueberries into the Instant Pot. Stir to combine.
2. Close the lid, select MANUAL, and cook at high pressure for 2 minutes.
3. When the cooking is complete, do a natural pressure release for 10 minutes. Quick release the remaining pressure.
4. Chill and serve.

Nutritional Information (Per Serving)
Calories: 94
Fat: 0.6 g
Sat Fat: 0.1 g
Carbohydrates: 23.2 g
Fiber: 3.3 g
Sugar: 17 g
Protein: 1.1 g
Sodium: 4 mg

Cashew Lemon Cheesecake

Serves: 4
Cooking Time: 20 minutes
Ingredients:
For crust:
½ cup quick cooking oats
¼ cup chopped dates, soaked in 2–3 tablespoons water for 30 minutes
¼ cup walnuts

For filling:
½ cup cashews, soaked in water for 3–4 hours
2 tablespoons coconut sugar
1 teaspoon lemon zest, grated
½ teaspoon vanilla extract
¼ cup coconut flour
¼ cup vanilla flavored coconut milk
1 tablespoon lemon juice
½ tablespoon arrowroot powder
¼ cup fresh blueberries

Directions:
1. Pour 1½ cups water in the Instant Pot. Place a steamer rack in it.

2. For crust: Add oats, dates and walnuts into a food processor and pulse until well combined. If the mixture is very dry, then add the soaked liquid of dates, a teaspoon at a timer and pulse each time. The mixture should be like dough that is slightly firm.

3. Take a springform pan that can fit in the instant pot. Grease with a little oil.

4. Transfer the mixture into the pan and use fingers to push the crust into the pan.

5. For the filling: Retain the cashew-soaked water and add cashews into the blender. Pour a little of the soaked water into the blender and blend until smooth.

6. Add coconut sugar, coconut flour, lemon zest, milk, vanilla extract and lemon juice into the blender and blend until smooth.

7. Add arrowroot powder into it and blend until smooth.

8. Spoon the mixture on top of the crust. Spread it evenly. Cover the dish with foil.

9. Place the dish on the rack.

10. Close the lid, select MANUAL, and cook at high pressure for 20 minutes.

11. When the timer goes off, let the pressure release naturally.

12. Remove the dish from the pot. Uncover and let it cool for a while.

13. Sprinkle the blueberries on top and let the cake cool completely.

14. Place in the refrigerator for at least 2–3 hours.

15. Slice into 4 wedges and serve.

Nutritional Information (Per Serving)
Calories: 346
Fat: 18.4 g
Sat Fat: 6.1 g
Carbohydrates: 41 g
Fiber: 9.6 g
Sugar: 15.7 g
Protein: 8.6 g
Sodium: 7 mg

Conclusion

I hope you enjoy the vegan Instant Pot recipes in this book. Make sure that your pantry is stocked with vegan ingredients so that the next time you are inviting your friends or family members for a meal, you can whip up delicious vegan food that'll make you feel like a gourmet chef.

Finally, I want to thank you for reading my book. If you enjoyed the book, please take the time to share your thoughts and post a review on the <u>Vegan Instant Pot Cookbook: Healthy and Delicious Plant-Based Recipes for Your Pressure Cooker</u> Amazon book page. It would be greatly appreciated!

Best wishes,

Jasmine King

Check Out My Other Books

Ketogenic Instant Pot Cookbook: Easy and Delicious
Ketogenic Recipes for Your Pressure Cooker
https://www.amazon.com/dp/B0791LTLWS/

Air Fryer Cookbook: Quick, Easy, and Healthy Recipes for
Your Air Fryer
https://www.amazon.com/Air-Fryer-Cookbook-Healthy-
Recipes-ebook/dp/B078L29KXC/

Anti Inflammatory Cookbook: Delicious Anti Inflammatory
Recipes to Fight Inflammation, Reduce Pain, and Restore
Your Overall Health
https://www.amazon.com/dp/B01N6R2HRY/

Clean Eating: 25 Best Clean Eating Recipes to Lose Weight
and Boost Your Energy
https://www.amazon.com/Clean-Eating-Recipes-Healthy-
Cookbook-ebook/dp/B01K4YX8H8/

DASH Diet: 25 Best DASH Diet Recipes for Lower Blood
Pressure and Weight Loss
https://www.amazon.com/DASH-Diet-Recipes-Pressure-
Cookbook-ebook/dp/B01KCQFDGM/

Green Smoothies: 40 Best Green Smoothie Recipes to Lose
Weight and Detox Your Body
https://www.amazon.com/Green-Smoothies-Smoothie-
Recipes-Weight-ebook/dp/B01KR7IYV2/

Paleo Diet: 25 Best Paleo Diet Recipes to Lose Weight and
Feel Energized
https://www.amazon.com/Paleo-Diet-Recipes-Weight-
Energized-ebook/dp/B01L38E3SW/

Mediterranean Diet: 25 Best Mediterranean Diet Recipes for Weight Loss and Healthy Eating
https://www.amazon.com/Mediterranean-Diet-Recipes-Weight-Healthy-ebook/dp/B01LE8Y24G/